The Book Lover's Companion

by
Jo Massaro

Date_____to_____

ISBN: 978-0-578-60077-2

Meet Jo

I fell in love with reading when I was in the seventh grade. My class assignment was to read *The Odyssey* by Homer. I thought the task was daunting.

To my surprise, I was reading and yearned for more. From that day forward, reading became my passion.

On our Christmas break, we were assigned to read *Gone with the Wind* by Margaret Mitchell. I remember Christmas morning, after all the presents were opened, and we filled our bellies with delights, I snuggled in bed and began reading.

I was transported into the history of the Civil War era and was drawn into the vivid characters and the spark-fly dialogue between Scarlett and Rhett. This began my love of history.

My passion for reading grew over my lifetime, and I have read hundreds of books. How I wished I had kept a record of each one. That is why I created this journal and hope it brings you many years of memories.

Happy reading. Jo

"Once you learn to read, you will be forever free".

- Frederick Douglas

Acknowledgements

This book would not have been possible without the encouragement of author and friend, PeggySue Wells. She has inspired and challenged me to take many steps of faith.

Kim Autrey, you have been a blessing to my life. Your words of wisdom and your great editing skills have made me a better writer. Thank you to my writer's group and your words of encouragement and suggestions.

To my daughter, Dianna, who has followed in my footsteps and loves to read. It's exciting for a parent to see their child fall in love with something that is near to their heart.

This book is dedicated to my husband, Dominick, who supports me in everything I put my hands too. He is a chef extraordinaire, and while I'm working, he provides a hot meal and so much more. I'm so grateful that God has put us together.

I encourage you to pass your love of reading on to our next generation. From the moment we touch a book, we take it out of hibernation and breathe life into it.

Above everything else, I dedicate this book to Jesus, who has shown me much grace and love. He taught me to embrace who I am with dignity and strength, as only He can.

My life is yours. Jo

Where is your favorite place to read?

☐ **in bed** ☐ **at home** ☐ **in the park** ☐ **on a train**
☐ **in my favorite chair** ☐ **on an airplane** ☐ **at the beach**
☐ **at a cafe**
☐ **other**_____

I love to read
☐ **at a slow pace** ☐ **at a medium pace**
☐ **at a quick pace**

If stranded on a desert island, I would like to have the following
books with me.

_____

_____

_____

My favorite genre is:

☐ **biography** ☐ **comedy** ☐ **historical fiction** ☐ **horror**
☐ **fiction** ☐ **non-fiction** ☐ **mystery** ☐ **poetry**
☐ **travel** ☐ **romance** ☐ **science fiction**
☐ **other**_____

You can never get a cup of tea large enough or a book long
enough to suit me.
– C.S. Lewis

Book Title: _____

Author: _____

Dated Started: _____ Date Finished: _____

Is this book part of a series? Yes ☐ No ☐

Category: ☐ Fiction ☐ Non-Fiction ☐ Biography
☐ Memoir ☐ Other _____

Rating: ✧✧✧✧✧

What did you love or not love about this book?

_____
_____
_____

If you could continue the story, where would you begin?

_____
_____
_____

Would you recommend this book? Why?

_____
_____
_____

What other book(s) do you want to read from this author?

_____

_____

_____

While reading, did you feel God was speaking to you in some way?

_____

_____

_____

_____

What scripture references do you want to remember? (Quote sentence, words or phrase.)

_____

_____

_____

_____

What character did you relate to and why?

_____

_____

_____

_____

Book Title: _____

Author: _____

Dated Started: _____ Date Finished: _____

Is this book part of a series? Yes ☐ No ☐

Category: ☐ Fiction ☐ Non-Fiction ☐ Biography
☐ Memoir ☐ Other _____

Rating: ✧✧✧✧✧

What did you love or not love about this book?

_____
_____
_____

If you could continue the story, where would you begin?

_____
_____
_____

Would you recommend this book? Why?

_____
_____
_____

What other book(s) do you want to read from this author?

_____

_____

_____

While reading, did you feel God was speaking to you in some way?

_____

_____

_____

_____

What scripture references do you want to remember?
(Quote sentence, words or phrase.)

_____

_____

_____

_____

What character did you relate to and why?

_____

_____

_____

_____

Book Title: _____

Author: _____

Dated Started: _____ Date Finished: _____

Is this book part of a series?   Yes ☐ No ☐

Category: ☐ Fiction ☐ Non-Fiction ☐ Biography
☐ Memoir ☐ Other _____

Rating: ✧✧✧✧✧

What did you love or not love about this book?
_____
_____
_____

If you could continue the story, where would you begin?
_____
_____
_____

Would you recommend this book? Why?
_____
_____
_____

What other book(s) do you want to read from this author?

_____

_____

_____

While reading, did you feel God was speaking to you in some way?

_____

_____

_____

_____

What scripture references do you want to remember?
(Quote sentence, words or phrase.)

_____

_____

_____

_____

What character did you relate to and why?

_____

_____

_____

_____

Book Title: _____

Author: _____

Dated Started: _____ Date Finished: _____

Is this book part of a series? Yes ☐ No ☐

Category: ☐ Fiction ☐ Non-Fiction ☐ Biography
☐ Memoir ☐ Other _____

Rating: ✧✧✧✧✧

What did you love or not love about this book?

_____
_____
_____

If you could continue the story, where would you begin?

_____
_____
_____

Would you recommend this book? Why?

_____
_____
_____

What other book(s) do you want to read from this author?

_____

_____

_____

While reading, did you feel God was speaking to you in some way?

_____

_____

_____

_____

What scripture references do you want to remember? (Quote sentence, words or phrase.)

_____

_____

_____

_____

What character did you relate to and why?

_____

_____

_____

_____

Book Title: _____

Author: _____

Dated Started: _____ Date Finished: _____

Is this book part of a series? Yes ☐ No ☐

Category: ☐ Fiction ☐ Non-Fiction ☐ Biography
☐ Memoir ☐ Other _____

Rating: ✧✧✧✧✧

What did you love or not love about this book?
_____
_____
_____

If you could continue the story, where would you begin?
_____
_____
_____

Would you recommend this book? Why?
_____
_____
_____

What other book(s) do you want to read from this author?

_____

_____

_____

While reading, did you feel God was speaking to you in some way?

_____

_____

_____

_____

What scripture references do you want to remember?
(Quote sentence, words or phrase.)

_____

_____

_____

_____

What character did you relate to and why?

_____

_____

_____

_____

Book Title: _____

Author: _____

Dated Started: _____ Date Finished: _____

Is this book part of a series? Yes ☐ No ☐

Category: ☐ Fiction ☐ Non-Fiction ☐ Biography
☐ Memoir ☐ Other _____

Rating: ✧✧✧✧

What did you love or not love about this book?
_____
_____
_____

If you could continue the story, where would you begin?
_____
_____
_____

Would you recommend this book? Why?
_____
_____
_____

What other book(s) do you want to read from this author?

_____

_____

_____

While reading, did you feel God was speaking to you in some way?

_____

_____

_____

_____

What scripture references do you want to remember? (Quote sentence, words or phrase.)

_____

_____

_____

_____

What character did you relate to and why?

_____

_____

_____

_____

Book Title: _____

Author: _____

Dated Started: _____ Date Finished: _____

Is this book part of a series? Yes ☐ No ☐

Category: ☐ Fiction ☐ Non-Fiction ☐ Biography
☐ Memoir ☐ Other_____

Rating: ✧✧✧✧

What did you love or not love about this book?
_____
_____
_____

If you could continue the story, where would you begin?
_____
_____
_____

Would you recommend this book? Why?
_____
_____
_____

What other book(s) do you want to read from this author?

_____

_____

_____

While reading, did you feel God was speaking to you in some way?

_____

_____

_____

_____

What scripture references do you want to remember?
(Quote sentence, words or phrase.)

_____

_____

_____

_____

What character did you relate to and why?

_____

_____

_____

_____

Book Title: _____

Author: _____

Dated Started: _____ Date Finished: _____

Is this book part of a series? Yes ☐ No ☐

Category: ☐ Fiction ☐ Non-Fiction ☐ Biography
☐ Memoir ☐ Other _____

Rating: ✧✧✧✧✧

What did you love or not love about this book?
_____
_____
_____

If you could continue the story, where would you begin?
_____
_____
_____

Would you recommend this book? Why?
_____
_____
_____

What other book(s) do you want to read from this author?

_____

_____

_____

While reading, did you feel God was speaking to you in some way?

_____

_____

_____

_____

What scripture references do you want to remember?
(Quote sentence, words or phrase.)

_____

_____

_____

_____

What character did you relate to and why?

_____

_____

_____

_____

Book Title: _____

Author: _____

Dated Started: _____ Date Finished: _____

Is this book part of a series? Yes ☐ No ☐

Category: ☐ Fiction ☐ Non-Fiction ☐ Biography
☐ Memoir ☐ Other _____

Rating: ✧✧✧✧✧

What did you love or not love about this book?
_____
_____
_____

If you could continue the story, where would you begin?
_____
_____
_____

Would you recommend this book? Why?
_____
_____
_____

What other book(s) do you want to read from this author?

_____

_____

_____

While reading, did you feel God was speaking to you in some way?

_____

_____

_____

_____

What scripture references do you want to remember?
(Quote sentence, words or phrase.)

_____

_____

_____

_____

What character did you relate to and why?

_____

_____

_____

_____

Book Title: _____

Author: _____

Dated Started: _____ Date Finished: _____

Is this book part of a series? Yes ☐ No ☐

Category: ☐ Fiction ☐ Non-Fiction ☐ Biography
☐ Memoir ☐ Other _____

Rating: ✧✧✧✧

What did you love or not love about this book?
_____
_____
_____

If you could continue the story, where would you begin?
_____
_____
_____

Would you recommend this book? Why?
_____
_____
_____

What other book(s) do you want to read from this author?

_____

_____

_____

While reading, did you feel God was speaking to you in some way?

_____

_____

_____

_____

What scripture references do you want to remember? (Quote sentence, words or phrase.)

_____

_____

_____

_____

What character did you relate to and why?

_____

_____

_____

_____

Book Title: _____

Author: _____

Dated Started: _____ Date Finished: _____

Is this book part of a series? Yes ☐ No ☐

Category: ☐ Fiction ☐ Non-Fiction ☐ Biography
☐ Memoir ☐ Other _____

Rating: ✧✧✧✧✧

What did you love or not love about this book?

_____
_____
_____

If you could continue the story, where would you begin?

_____
_____
_____

Would you recommend this book? Why?

_____
_____
_____

What other book(s) do you want to read from this author?

_____

_____

_____

While reading, did you feel God was speaking to you in some way?

_____

_____

_____

_____

What scripture references do you want to remember?
(Quote sentence, words or phrase.)

_____

_____

_____

_____

What character did you relate to and why?

_____

_____

_____

_____

Book Title: _____

Author: _____

Dated Started: _____ Date Finished: _____

Is this book part of a series? Yes ☐ No ☐

Category: ☐ Fiction ☐ Non-Fiction ☐ Biography
☐ Memoir ☐ Other _____

Rating: ✧✧✧✧✧

What did you love or not love about this book?
_____
_____
_____

If you could continue the story, where would you begin?
_____
_____
_____

Would you recommend this book? Why?
_____
_____
_____

What other book(s) do you want to read from this author?

_____

_____

_____

While reading, did you feel God was speaking to you in some
way?

_____

_____

_____

_____

What scripture references do you want to remember?
(Quote sentence, words or phrase.)

_____

_____

_____

_____

What character did you relate to and why?

_____

_____

_____

_____

Book Title: _____

Author: _____

Dated Started: _____ Date Finished: _____

Is this book part of a series? Yes ☐ No ☐

Category: ☐ Fiction ☐ Non-Fiction ☐ Biography
☐ Memoir ☐ Other _____

Rating: ✧✧✧✧✧

What did you love or not love about this book?

_____
_____
_____

If you could continue the story, where would you begin?

_____
_____
_____

Would you recommend this book? Why?

_____
_____
_____

What other book(s) do you want to read from this author?

_____
_____
_____

While reading, did you feel God was speaking to you in some way?

_____
_____
_____
_____

What scripture references do you want to remember?
(Quote sentence, words or phrase.)

_____
_____
_____
_____

What character did you relate to and why?

_____
_____
_____
_____

Book Title: _____

Author: _____

Dated Started: _____ Date Finished: _____

Is this book part of a series? Yes ☐ No ☐

Category: ☐ Fiction ☐ Non-Fiction ☐ Biography
☐ Memoir ☐ Other _____

Rating: ✧✧✧✧

What did you love or not love about this book?
_____
_____
_____

If you could continue the story, where would you begin?
_____
_____
_____

Would you recommend this book? Why?
_____
_____
_____

What other book(s) do you want to read from this author?

_____

_____

_____

While reading, did you feel God was speaking to you in some way?

_____

_____

_____

_____

What scripture references do you want to remember? (Quote sentence, words or phrase.)

_____

_____

_____

_____

What character did you relate to and why?

_____

_____

_____

_____

Book Title: _____

Author: _____

Dated Started: _____ Date Finished: _____

Is this book part of a series? Yes ☐ No ☐

Category: ☐ Fiction ☐ Non-Fiction ☐ Biography
☐ Memoir ☐ Other _____

Rating: ✧✧✧✧✧

What did you love or not love about this book?

_____

_____

_____

If you could continue the story, where would you begin?

_____

_____

_____

Would you recommend this book? Why?

_____

_____

_____

What other book(s) do you want to read from this author?

_____

_____

_____

While reading, did you feel God was speaking to you in some way?

_____

_____

_____

_____

What scripture references do you want to remember?
(Quote sentence, words or phrase.)

_____

_____

_____

_____

What character did you relate to and why?

_____

_____

_____

_____

Book Title: _____

Author: _____

Dated Started: _____ Date Finished: _____

Is this book part of a series? Yes ☐ No ☐

Category: ☐ Fiction ☐ Non-Fiction ☐ Biography
☐ Memoir ☐ Other _____

Rating: ✧✧✧✧✧

What did you love or not love about this book?

_____

_____

_____

If you could continue the story, where would you begin?

_____

_____

_____

Would you recommend this book? Why?

_____

_____

_____

What other book(s) do you want to read from this author?

_____

_____

_____

While reading, did you feel God was speaking to you in some way?

_____

_____

_____

_____

What scripture references do you want to remember? (Quote sentence, words or phrase.)

_____

_____

_____

_____

What character did you relate to and why?

_____

_____

_____

_____

Book Title: _____

Author: _____

Dated Started: _____ Date Finished: _____

Is this book part of a series? Yes ☐ No ☐

Category: ☐ Fiction ☐ Non-Fiction ☐ Biography
☐ Memoir ☐ Other _____

Rating: ✧✧✧✧✧

What did you love or not love about this book?
_____
_____
_____

If you could continue the story, where would you begin?
_____
_____
_____

Would you recommend this book? Why?
_____
_____
_____

What other book(s) do you want to read from this author?

_____

_____

_____

While reading, did you feel God was speaking to you in some way?

_____

_____

_____

_____

What scripture references do you want to remember?
(Quote sentence, words or phrase.)

_____

_____

_____

What character did you relate to and why?

_____

_____

_____

_____

Book Title: _____

Author: _____

Dated Started: _____ Date Finished: _____

Is this book part of a series? Yes ☐ No ☐

Category: ☐ Fiction ☐ Non-Fiction ☐ Biography
☐ Memoir ☐ Other _____

Rating: ✧✧✧✧

What did you love or not love about this book?
_____
_____
_____

If you could continue the story, where would you begin?
_____
_____
_____

Would you recommend this book? Why?
_____
_____
_____

What other book(s) do you want to read from this author?

_____

_____

_____

While reading, did you feel God was speaking to you in some way?

_____

_____

_____

_____

What scripture references do you want to remember? (Quote sentence, words or phrase.)

_____

_____

_____

_____

What character did you relate to and why?

_____

_____

_____

Book Title: _____

Author: _____

Dated Started: _____ Date Finished: _____

Is this book part of a series? Yes ☐ No ☐

Category: ☐ Fiction ☐ Non-Fiction ☐ Biography
☐ Memoir ☐ Other_____

Rating: ✧✧✧✧

What did you love or not love about this book?
_____
_____
_____

If you could continue the story, where would you begin?
_____
_____
_____

Would you recommend this book? Why?
_____
_____
_____

What other book(s) do you want to read from this author?

_____

_____

_____

While reading, did you feel God was speaking to you in some way?

_____

_____

_____

_____

What scripture references do you want to remember? (Quote sentence, words or phrase.)

_____

_____

_____

_____

What character did you relate to and why?

_____

_____

_____

_____

Book Title: _____

Author: _____

Dated Started: _____ Date Finished: _____

Is this book part of a series? Yes ☐ No ☐

Category: ☐ Fiction ☐ Non-Fiction ☐ Biography
☐ Memoir ☐ Other _____

Rating: ✧✧✧✧

What did you love or not love about this book?
_____
_____
_____

If you could continue the story, where would you begin?
_____
_____
_____

Would you recommend this book? Why?
_____
_____

What other book(s) do you want to read from this author?

_____

_____

_____

While reading, did you feel God was speaking to you in some way?

_____

_____

_____

_____

What scripture references do you want to remember? (Quote sentence, words or phrase.)

_____

_____

_____

_____

What character did you relate to and why?

_____

_____

_____

_____

Book Title: _____

Author: _____

Dated Started: _____ Date Finished: _____

Is this book part of a series? Yes ☐ No ☐

Category: ☐ Fiction ☐ Non-Fiction ☐ Biography
☐ Memoir ☐ Other _____

Rating: ✧✧✧✧✧

What did you love or not love about this book?

_____
_____
_____

If you could continue the story, where would you begin?

_____
_____
_____

Would you recommend this book? Why?

_____
_____
_____

What other book(s) do you want to read from this author?

_____

_____

_____

While reading, did you feel God was speaking to you in some way?

_____

_____

_____

_____

What scripture references do you want to remember?
(Quote sentence, words or phrase.)

_____

_____

_____

_____

What character did you relate to and why?

_____

_____

_____

_____

Book Title: _____

Author: _____

Dated Started: _____ Date Finished: _____

Is this book part of a series? Yes ☐ No ☐

Category: ☐ Fiction ☐ Non-Fiction ☐ Biography
☐ Memoir ☐ Other _____

Rating: ✧✧✧✧✧

What did you love or not love about this book?
_____
_____
_____

If you could continue the story, where would you begin?
_____
_____
_____

Would you recommend this book? Why?
_____
_____
_____

What other book(s) do you want to read from this author?

_____

_____

_____

While reading, did you feel God was speaking to you in some way?

_____

_____

_____

_____

What scripture references do you want to remember?
(Quote sentence, words or phrase.)

_____

_____

_____

_____

What character did you relate to and why?

_____

_____

_____

_____

Book Title: _____

Author: _____

Dated Started: _____ Date Finished: _____

Is this book part of a series? Yes ☐ No ☐

Category: ☐ Fiction ☐ Non-Fiction ☐ Biography
☐ Memoir ☐ Other _____

Rating: ✧✧✧✧

What did you love or not love about this book?
_____
_____
_____

If you could continue the story, where would you begin?
_____
_____
_____

Would you recommend this book? Why?
_____
_____
_____

What other book(s) do you want to read from this author?

_____

_____

_____

While reading, did you feel God was speaking to you in some way?

_____

_____

_____

_____

What scripture references do you want to remember? (Quote sentence, words or phrase.)

_____

_____

_____

_____

What character did you relate to and why?

_____

_____

_____

_____

Book Title: _____

Author: _____

Dated Started: _____ Date Finished: _____

Is this book part of a series? Yes ☐ No ☐

Category: ☐ Fiction ☐ Non-Fiction ☐ Biography
☐ Memoir ☐ Other _____

Rating: ✧✧✧✧✧

What did you love or not love about this book?
_____
_____
_____

If you could continue the story, where would you begin?
_____
_____
_____

Would you recommend this book? Why?
_____
_____
_____

What other book(s) do you want to read from this author?

_____

_____

_____

While reading, did you feel God was speaking to you in some way?

_____

_____

_____

_____

What scripture references do you want to remember?
(Quote sentence, words or phrase.)

_____

_____

_____

_____

What character did you relate to and why?

_____

_____

_____

_____

Book Title: _____

Author: _____

Dated Started: _____ Date Finished: _____

Is this book part of a series?   Yes ☐ No ☐

Category: ☐ Fiction ☐ Non-Fiction ☐ Biography
☐ Memoir ☐ Other_____

Rating: ✧✧✧✧

What did you love or not love about this book?
_____
_____
_____

If you could continue the story, where would you begin?
_____
_____
_____

Would you recommend this book? Why?
_____
_____
_____

What other book(s) do you want to read from this author?

_____

_____

_____

While reading, did you feel God was speaking to you in some way?

_____

_____

_____

_____

What scripture references do you want to remember? (Quote sentence, words or phrase.)

_____

_____

_____

_____

What character did you relate to and why?

_____

_____

_____

_____

Book Title: _____

Author: _____

Dated Started: _____ Date Finished: _____

Is this book part of a series? Yes ☐ No ☐

Category: ☐ Fiction ☐ Non-Fiction ☐ Biography
☐ Memoir ☐ Other _____

Rating: ✧✧✧✧

What did you love or not love about this book?
_____
_____
_____

If you could continue the story, where would you begin?
_____
_____
_____

Would you recommend this book? Why?
_____
_____
_____

What other book(s) do you want to read from this author?

_____

_____

_____

While reading, did you feel God was speaking to you in some way?

_____

_____

_____

_____

What scripture references do you want to remember?
(Quote sentence, words or phrase.)

_____

_____

_____

_____

What character did you relate to and why?

_____

_____

_____

_____

Book Title: _____

Author: _____

Dated Started: _____ Date Finished: _____

Is this book part of a series? Yes ☐ No ☐

Category: ☐ Fiction ☐ Non-Fiction ☐ Biography
☐ Memoir ☐ Other _____

Rating: ✧✧✧✧✧

What did you love or not love about this book?
_____
_____
_____

If you could continue the story, where would you begin?
_____
_____
_____

Would you recommend this book? Why?
_____
_____
_____

What other book(s) do you want to read from this author?

_____

_____

_____

While reading, did you feel God was speaking to you in some way?

_____

_____

_____

_____

What scripture references do you want to remember? (Quote sentence, words or phrase.)

_____

_____

_____

_____

What character did you relate to and why?

_____

_____

_____

_____

Book Title: _____

Author: _____

Dated Started: _____ Date Finished: _____

Is this book part of a series? Yes ☐ No ☐

Category: ☐ Fiction ☐ Non-Fiction ☐ Biography
☐ Memoir ☐ Other _____

Rating: ✧✧✧✧

What did you love or not love about this book?
_____
_____
_____

If you could continue the story, where would you begin?
_____
_____
_____

Would you recommend this book? Why?
_____
_____
_____

What other book(s) do you want to read from this author?

_____

_____

_____

While reading, did you feel God was speaking to you in some way?

_____

_____

_____

_____

What scripture references do you want to remember?
(Quote sentence, words or phrase.)

_____

_____

_____

What character did you relate to and why?

_____

_____

_____

_____

Book Title: _____

Author: _____

Dated Started: _____ Date Finished: _____

Is this book part of a series? Yes ☐ No ☐

Category: ☐ Fiction ☐ Non-Fiction ☐ Biography
☐ Memoir ☐ Other _____

Rating: ✧✧✧✧

What did you love or not love about this book?

_____

_____

_____

If you could continue the story, where would you begin?

_____

_____

_____

Would you recommend this book? Why?

_____

_____

_____

What other book(s) do you want to read from this author?

_____

_____

_____

While reading, did you feel God was speaking to you in some way?

_____

_____

_____

_____

What scripture references do you want to remember?
(Quote sentence, words or phrase.)

_____

_____

_____

_____

What character did you relate to and why?

_____

_____

_____

_____

Book Title: _____

Author: _____

Dated Started: _____ Date Finished: _____

Is this book part of a series? Yes ☐ No ☐

Category: ☐ Fiction ☐ Non-Fiction ☐ Biography
☐ Memoir ☐ Other _____

Rating: ✧✧✧✧✧

What did you love or not love about this book?
_____
_____
_____

If you could continue the story, where would you begin?
_____
_____
_____

Would you recommend this book? Why?
_____
_____

What other book(s) do you want to read from this author?

_____

_____

_____

While reading, did you feel God was speaking to you in some way?

_____

_____

_____

_____

What scripture references do you want to remember?
(Quote sentence, words or phrase.)

_____

_____

_____

_____

What character did you relate to and why?

_____

_____

_____

_____

Book Title: _____

Author: _____

Dated Started: _____ Date Finished: _____

Is this book part of a series? Yes ☐ No ☐

Category: ☐ Fiction ☐ Non-Fiction ☐ Biography
☐ Memoir ☐ Other_____

Rating: ✧✧✧✧

What did you love or not love about this book?
_____
_____
_____

If you could continue the story, where would you begin?
_____
_____
_____

Would you recommend this book? Why?
_____
_____
_____

What other book(s) do you want to read from this author?

_____

_____

_____

While reading, did you feel God was speaking to you in some way?

_____

_____

_____

_____

What scripture references do you want to remember? (Quote sentence, words or phrase.)

_____

_____

_____

_____

What character did you relate to and why?

_____

_____

_____

_____

Book Title: _____

Author: _____

Dated Started: _____ Date Finished: _____

Is this book part of a series? Yes ☐ No ☐

Category: ☐ Fiction ☐ Non-Fiction ☐ Biography
☐ Memoir ☐ Other _____

Rating: ✦✦✦✦

What did you love or not love about this book?
_____
_____
_____

If you could continue the story, where would you begin?
_____
_____
_____

Would you recommend this book? Why?
_____
_____
_____

What other book(s) do you want to read from this author?

_____

_____

_____

While reading, did you feel God was speaking to you in some way?

_____

_____

_____

_____

What scripture references do you want to remember?
(Quote sentence, words or phrase.)

_____

_____

_____

_____

What character did you relate to and why?

_____

_____

_____

_____

Book Title: _____

Author: _____

Dated Started: _____ Date Finished: _____

Is this book part of a series? Yes ☐ No ☐

Category: ☐ Fiction ☐ Non-Fiction ☐ Biography
☐ Memoir ☐ Other _____

Rating: ✧✧✧✧✧

What did you love or not love about this book?
_____
_____
_____

If you could continue the story, where would you begin?
_____
_____
_____

Would you recommend this book? Why?
_____
_____
_____

What other book(s) do you want to read from this author?

_____

_____

_____

While reading, did you feel God was speaking to you in some way?

_____

_____

_____

_____

What scripture references do you want to remember? (Quote sentence, words or phrase.)

_____

_____

_____

_____

What character did you relate to and why?

_____

_____

_____

_____

Book Title: _____

Author: _____

Dated Started: _____ Date Finished: _____

Is this book part of a series?   Yes ☐ No ☐

Category: ☐ Fiction ☐ Non-Fiction ☐ Biography
☐ Memoir ☐ Other _____

Rating: ✧✧✧✧

What did you love or not love about this book?
_____
_____
_____

If you could continue the story, where would you begin?
_____
_____
_____

Would you recommend this book? Why?
_____
_____
_____

What other book(s) do you want to read from this author?

_____

_____

_____

While reading, did you feel God was speaking to you in some way?

_____

_____

_____

_____

What scripture references do you want to remember? (Quote sentence, words or phrase.)

_____

_____

_____

_____

What character did you relate to and why?

_____

_____

_____

_____

Book Title: _____

Author: _____

Dated Started: _____ Date Finished: _____

Is this book part of a series?   Yes ☐   No ☐

Category: ☐ Fiction ☐ Non-Fiction ☐ Biography
☐ Memoir ☐ Other _____

Rating: ✧✧✧✧

What did you love or not love about this book?
_____
_____
_____

If you could continue the story, where would you begin?
_____
_____
_____

Would you recommend this book? Why?
_____
_____
_____

What other book(s) do you want to read from this author?

_____

_____

_____

While reading, did you feel God was speaking to you in some
way?

_____

_____

_____

_____

What scripture references do you want to remember?
(Quote sentence, words or phrase.)

_____

_____

_____

What character did you relate to and why?

_____

_____

_____

_____

Book Title: _____

Author: _____

Dated Started: _____ Date Finished: _____

Is this book part of a series? Yes ☐ No ☐

Category: ☐ Fiction ☐ Non-Fiction ☐ Biography
☐ Memoir ☐ Other_____

Rating: ✧✧✧✧✧

What did you love or not love about this book?
_____
_____
_____

If you could continue the story, where would you begin?
_____
_____
_____

Would you recommend this book? Why?
_____
_____
_____

What other book(s) do you want to read from this author?

_____

_____

_____

While reading, did you feel God was speaking to you in some way?

_____

_____

_____

What scripture references do you want to remember? (Quote sentence, words or phrase.)

_____

_____

_____

What character did you relate to and why?

_____

_____

_____

_____

Book Title: _____

Author: _____

Dated Started: _____ Date Finished: _____

Is this book part of a series? Yes ☐ No ☐

Category: ☐ Fiction ☐ Non-Fiction ☐ Biography
☐ Memoir ☐ Other _____

Rating: ✧✧✧✧✧

What did you love or not love about this book?
_____
_____
_____

If you could continue the story, where would you begin?
_____
_____
_____

Would you recommend this book? Why?
_____
_____
_____

What other book(s) do you want to read from this author?

_____

_____

_____

While reading, did you feel God was speaking to you in some way?

_____

_____

_____

_____

What scripture references do you want to remember? (Quote sentence, words or phrase.)

_____

_____

_____

_____

What character did you relate to and why?

_____

_____

_____

_____

Book Title: _____

Author: _____

Dated Started: _____ Date Finished: _____

Is this book part of a series? Yes ☐ No ☐

Category: ☐ Fiction ☐ Non-Fiction ☐ Biography
☐ Memoir ☐ Other _____

Rating: ✧✧✧✧

What did you love or not love about this book?
_____
_____
_____

If you could continue the story, where would you begin?
_____
_____
_____

Would you recommend this book? Why?
_____
_____
_____

What other book(s) do you want to read from this author?

_____

_____

_____

While reading, did you feel God was speaking to you in some way?

_____

_____

_____

_____

What scripture references do you want to remember? (Quote sentence, words or phrase.)

_____

_____

_____

_____

What character did you relate to and why?

_____

_____

_____

_____

Book Title: _____

Author: _____

Dated Started: _____ Date Finished: _____

Is this book part of a series? Yes ☐ No ☐

Category: ☐ Fiction ☐ Non-Fiction ☐ Biography
☐ Memoir ☐ Other _____

Rating: ✧✧✧✧

What did you love or not love about this book?
_____
_____
_____

If you could continue the story, where would you begin?
_____
_____
_____

Would you recommend this book? Why?
_____
_____
_____

What other book(s) do you want to read from this author?

_____

_____

_____

While reading, did you feel God was speaking to you in some way?

_____

_____

_____

_____

What scripture references do you want to remember?
(Quote sentence, words or phrase.)

_____

_____

_____

_____

What character did you relate to and why?

_____

_____

_____

_____

Book Title: _____

Author: _____

Dated Started: _____ Date Finished: _____

Is this book part of a series? Yes ☐ No ☐

Category: ☐ Fiction ☐ Non-Fiction ☐ Biography
☐ Memoir ☐ Other_____

Rating: ✧✧✧✧

What did you love or not love about this book?
_____
_____
_____

If you could continue the story, where would you begin?
_____
_____
_____

Would you recommend this book? Why?
_____
_____
_____

What other book(s) do you want to read from this author?

_____

_____

_____

While reading, did you feel God was speaking to you in some way?

_____

_____

_____

What scripture references do you want to remember? (Quote sentence, words or phrase.)

_____

_____

_____

What character did you relate to and why?

_____

_____

_____

Book Title: _____

Author: _____

Dated Started: _____ Date Finished: _____

Is this book part of a series? Yes ☐ No ☐

Category: ☐ Fiction ☐ Non-Fiction ☐ Biography
☐ Memoir ☐ Other _____

Rating: ✧✧✧✧✧

What did you love or not love about this book?

_____
_____
_____

If you could continue the story, where would you begin?

_____
_____
_____

Would you recommend this book? Why?

_____
_____
_____

What other book(s) do you want to read from this author?

_____

_____

_____

While reading, did you feel God was speaking to you in some
way?

_____

_____

_____

_____

What scripture references do you want to remember?
(Quote sentence, words or phrase.)

_____

_____

_____

_____

What character did you relate to and why?

_____

_____

_____

_____

Book Title: _____

Author: _____

Dated Started: _____ Date Finished: _____

Is this book part of a series?   Yes ☐ No ☐

Category: ☐ Fiction ☐ Non-Fiction ☐ Biography
☐ Memoir ☐ Other _____

Rating: ✧✧✧✧✧

What did you love or not love about this book?
_____
_____
_____

If you could continue the story, where would you begin?
_____
_____
_____

Would you recommend this book? Why?
_____
_____
_____

What other book(s) do you want to read from this author?

_____

_____

_____

While reading, did you feel God was speaking to you in some way?

_____

_____

_____

_____

What scripture references do you want to remember?
(Quote sentence, words or phrase.)

_____

_____

_____

What character did you relate to and why?

_____

_____

_____

_____

Book Title: _____

Author: _____

Dated Started: _____ Date Finished: _____

Is this book part of a series? Yes ☐ No ☐

Category: ☐ Fiction ☐ Non-Fiction ☐ Biography
☐ Memoir ☐ Other _____

Rating: ✧✧✧✧✧

What did you love or not love about this book?
_____
_____
_____

If you could continue the story, where would you begin?
_____
_____
_____

Would you recommend this book? Why?
_____
_____
_____

What other book(s) do you want to read from this author?

_____

_____

_____

While reading, did you feel God was speaking to you in some way?

_____

_____

_____

_____

What scripture references do you want to remember? (Quote sentence, words or phrase.)

_____

_____

_____

_____

What character did you relate to and why?

_____

_____

_____

_____

Book Title: _____

Author: _____

Dated Started: _____ Date Finished: _____

Is this book part of a series? Yes ☐ No ☐

Category: ☐ Fiction ☐ Non-Fiction ☐ Biography
☐ Memoir ☐ Other _____

Rating: ✧✧✧✧✧ .

What did you love or not love about this book?
_____
_____
_____

If you could continue the story, where would you begin?
_____
_____
_____

Would you recommend this book? Why?
_____
_____
_____

What other book(s) do you want to read from this author?

_____

_____

_____

While reading, did you feel God was speaking to you in some way?

_____

_____

_____

_____

What scripture references do you want to remember? (Quote sentence, words or phrase.)

_____

_____

_____

_____

What character did you relate to and why?

_____

_____

_____

_____

Book Title: _____

Author: _____

Dated Started: _____ Date Finished: _____

Is this book part of a series? Yes ☐ No ☐

Category: ☐ Fiction ☐ Non-Fiction ☐ Biography
☐ Memoir ☐ Other _____

Rating: ✧✧✧✧

What did you love or not love about this book?
_____
_____
_____

If you could continue the story, where would you begin?
_____
_____
_____

Would you recommend this book? Why?
_____
_____
_____

What other book(s) do you want to read from this author?

_____

_____

_____

While reading, did you feel God was speaking to you in some way?

_____

_____

_____

_____

What scripture references do you want to remember? (Quote sentence, words or phrase.)

_____

_____

_____

_____

What character did you relate to and why?

_____

_____

_____

_____

Book Title: _____

Author: _____

Dated Started: _____ Date Finished: _____

Is this book part of a series? Yes ☐ No ☐

Category: ☐ Fiction ☐ Non-Fiction ☐ Biography
☐ Memoir ☐ Other _____

Rating: ✧✧✧✧✧

What did you love or not love about this book?

_____
_____
_____

If you could continue the story, where would you begin?

_____
_____
_____

Would you recommend this book? Why?

_____
_____
_____

What other book(s) do you want to read from this author?

_____

_____

_____

While reading, did you feel God was speaking to you in some way?

_____

_____

_____

_____

What scripture references do you want to remember?
(Quote sentence, words or phrase.)

_____

_____

_____

_____

What character did you relate to and why?

_____

_____

_____

_____

Book Title: _____

Author: _____

Dated Started: _____ Date Finished: _____

Is this book part of a series? Yes ☐ No ☐

Category: ☐ Fiction ☐ Non-Fiction ☐ Biography
☐ Memoir ☐ Other _____

Rating: ✧✧✧✧✧

What did you love or not love about this book?
_____
_____
_____

If you could continue the story, where would you begin?
_____
_____
_____

Would you recommend this book? Why?
_____
_____
_____

What other book(s) do you want to read from this author?

_____

_____

_____

While reading, did you feel God was speaking to you in some way?

_____

_____

_____

_____

What scripture references do you want to remember? (Quote sentence, words or phrase.)

_____

_____

_____

_____

What character did you relate to and why?

_____

_____

_____

_____

Book Title: _____

Author: _____

Dated Started: _____ Date Finished: _____

Is this book part of a series? Yes ☐ No ☐

Category: ☐ Fiction ☐ Non-Fiction ☐ Biography
☐ Memoir ☐ Other _____

Rating: ✧✧✧✧

What did you love or not love about this book?
_____
_____
_____

If you could continue the story, where would you begin?
_____
_____
_____

Would you recommend this book? Why?
_____
_____
_____

What other book(s) do you want to read from this author?

_____

_____

_____

While reading, did you feel God was speaking to you in some way?

_____

_____

_____

_____

What scripture references do you want to remember? (Quote sentence, words or phrase.)

_____

_____

_____

_____

What character did you relate to and why?

_____

_____

_____

_____

Book Title: _____

Author: _____

Dated Started: _____ Date Finished: _____

Is this book part of a series? Yes ☐ No ☐

Category: ☐ Fiction ☐ Non-Fiction ☐ Biography
☐ Memoir ☐ Other _____

Rating: ✧✧✧✧

What did you love or not love about this book?
_____
_____
_____

If you could continue the story, where would you begin?
_____
_____
_____

Would you recommend this book? Why?
_____
_____
_____

What other book(s) do you want to read from this author?

_____

_____

_____

While reading, did you feel God was speaking to you in some way?

_____

_____

_____

_____

What scripture references do you want to remember? (Quote sentence, words or phrase.)

_____

_____

_____

What character did you relate to and why?

_____

_____

_____

_____

Books I Want to Read

<u>*Books*</u>   <u>*Authors*</u>

_____

_____

_____

_____

_____

_____

_____

_____

_____

_____

_____

_____

_____

_____

_____

*Rainy days should be spent at home with a cup of tea
and a good book.
-Bill Watterson*

Books I Want to Read

Books   _Authors_

_____

_____

_____

_____

_____

_____

_____

_____

_____

_____

_____

_____

_____

_____

_____

_____

_Rainy days should be spent at home with a cup of tea
and a good book.
-Bill Watterson_

Books I Want to Read

Books   Authors

_____

_____

_____

_____

_____

_____

_____

_____

_____

_____

_____

_____

Rainy days should be spent at home with a cup of tea
and a good book.
-Bill Watterson

Books I Want to Read

Books   _Authors_

_**Rainy days should be spent at home with a cup of tea
and a good book.
-Bill Watterson**_

Book Signing Events

Date: _____

Author: _____

Book: _____

Place: _____

Moments I want to remember:

_____

_____

_____

_____

PHOTO

Book Signing Events

Date: _____

Author: _____

Book: _____

Place: _____

Moments I want to remember:

_____

_____

_____

_____

PHOTO

Book Signing Events

Date: _____

Author: _____

Book: _____

Place: _____

Moments I want to remember:

_____

_____

_____

_____

PHOTO

Book Signing Events

Date: _____

Author: _____

Book: _____

Place: _____

Moments I want to remember:

_____

_____

_____

_____

PHOTO

Borrowed Books

Book	From	Returned

I declare after all there is no enjoyment like reading! How much sooner one tires of anything than of a book! When I have a house of my own, I shall be miserable if I have not an excellent library.
– Jane Austen

Borrowed Books

Book	_From_	_Returned_

I declare after all there is no enjoyment like reading! How much sooner one tires of anything than of a book! When I have a house of my own, I shall be miserable if I have not an excellent library.
– Jane Austen

Borrowed Books

Book	From	Returned

I declare after all there is no enjoyment like reading! How much sooner one tires of anything than of a book! When I have a house of my own, I shall be miserable if I have not an excellent library.
— Jane Austen

Borrowed Books

Book	From	Returned

I declare after all there is no enjoyment like reading! How much sooner one tires of anything than of a book! When I have a house of my own, I shall be miserable if I have not an excellent library.
– Jane Austen

Borrowed Books

Book	From	Returned

I declare after all there is no enjoyment like reading! How much sooner one tires of anything than of a book! When I have a house of my own, I shall be miserable if I have not an excellent library.
— Jane Austen

Borrowed Books

Book	From	Returned

I declare after all there is no enjoyment like reading! How much sooner one tires of anything than of a book! When I have a house of my own, I shall be miserable if I have not an excellent library.
— Jane Austen

Loaned Books

Book	_To_	_Returned_

Fill your house with stacks of books,
in all the crannies and all the nooks.
– Dr. Seuss

Loaned Books

Book	_To_	_Returned_

Fill your house with stacks of books,
in all the crannies and all the nooks.
– Dr. Seuss

Loaned Books

Book	To	Returned

Fill your house with stacks of books,
in all the crannies and all the nooks.
— Dr. Seuss

Loaned Books

Book	To	Returned

Fill your house with stacks of books,
in all the crannies and all the nooks.
— Dr. Seuss

Book Club Reading List

Book Club I belong to:

_____

_____

Date   *Book and Author*

_____

_____

_____

_____

_____

_____

_____

_____

_____

_____

_____

_____

_____

_____

_____

_____

_____

_____

_____

Books are not made for furniture, but there is nothing else that so beautifully furnishes a house.
– Henry Ward Beecher

Book Club Reading List

Book Club I belong to:

_____

_____

Date   Book and Author

_____
_____
_____
_____
_____
_____
_____
_____
_____
_____
_____
_____
_____
_____
_____
_____
_____
_____
_____

Books are not made for furniture, but there is nothing else that so beautifully furnishes a house.
— Henry Ward Beecher

Calling all Authors

Writer's groups I belong to: _____
_____

Do you have an idea for a book, magazine article, blog?

Write your thoughts below.

_____
_____
_____
_____
_____
_____
_____
_____
_____
_____
_____
_____
_____
_____
_____
_____
_____
_____

There is more treasure in books than in all the pirate's
loot on Treasure Island.
– Walt Disney

Calling all Authors

Writer's groups I belong to: _____
_____

Do you have an idea for a book, magazine article, blog?

Write your thoughts below.

_____
_____
_____
_____
_____
_____
_____
_____
_____
_____
_____
_____
_____
_____
_____
_____
_____
_____
_____

There is more treasure in books than in all the pirate's
loot on Treasure Island.
— Walt Disney

Calling all Authors

Writer's groups I belong to: _____

_____

Do you have an idea for a book, magazine article, blog?

Write your thoughts below.

_____
_____
_____
_____
_____
_____
_____
_____
_____
_____
_____
_____
_____
_____
_____
_____
_____
_____

There is more treasure in books than in all the pirate's
loot on Treasure Island.
– Walt Disney

About the Author

Jo is founder and curator of Yahweh Sisterhood Book Club. The club meets the first Thursday of each month where you not only have the opportunity to read the book but also get to meet the author either in person or through Facebook or Zoom.

Speaker

Jo brings humor, energy, authenticity, faith, and strength she found in the Word of God to her presentations.

She describes her journey through her darkest times and how God brought her to a relationship with the Light of the World.

She offers themed messages to your group and works with your team to customize a topic you have selected. She speaks before small or large groups, churches, or wherever God leads her.

For further information:

Book Club
      Website: www.yahwehsisterhoodbookclub.com
      Facebook: Yahweh Sisterhood Book Club FW

Contact Jo
      Email: jomassarospeaker@gmail.com
      Facebook: Jo Massaro

CPSIA information can be obtained
at www.ICGtesting.com
Printed in the USA
BVHW041352141119
563849BV00006B/232/P

9 780578 600772